Feeding Hour

Feeding Hour

Poems by Jessica Gigot

Trail to Table Press
Eastsound, WA

Library of Congress Cataloguing-in-Publication Data available.

First Edition
Poetry
ISBN: 978-0-578-71461-5

Cover Art: "Dish Towel" copyright Margaret Davidson 2019,
courtesy of i.e. gallery, Edison, WA

Author Photo: Steve Johnston

Trail to Table is an imprint of Wandering Aengus Press.
We are dedicated to publishing works to enrich lives and make
the world a better place.

Wandering Aengus Press
PO Box 334, Eastsound, WA 98245
trailtotable.net
wanderingaenguspress.com

Contents

III. familial truths

IV. mothering

For Bertha and Ruth

I. birth stories

FLEECE

The sheep are shorn
two times a year.

In fall, steam rises
from white, now slender

bodies that huddle together
bare shoulder to bare shoulder.

By now each belly is full of new life.
Without a half year's worth of wool

we can measure the swell of each ewe
as she matures toward motherhood.

Their lanolin soaked fleeces
are clouds piled in the barn

waiting to be cleaned and carded
and spun into yarn. We celebrate

this wonder, fiber transformed from grass,
mindful that another season has passed.

LATCH

for Jeanine

The lamb, four minutes old
stumbles toward the scent
of safety, vacant womb.
Lurking in barn shadows,
I hesitate to intervene
believing this nascent soul
will find its way.

The lamb, forty minutes old
stands and knocks the bag
with a steady jolt.
Despite the wet chill
of March and amniotic fluid
mouth discovers milk.

I come back to the house
before dawn to warm up.
In the privacy of a shower
I circle my tender, dark areolae
now larger than silver dollars.

When you finally arrive, I hope
you latch on to me without fear.
Let me nourish you
with all the flavor
my world can offer.

FETAL MOVEMENT

These fluttering movements feel like monarchs
Trapped inside me. My stomach is a mason jar
Holding this black and orange verve.

I remember watching their wings cling
To oyamel fir trees, *Abies religiosa*, after two
Thousand miles of flight. Generations four
Times removed return to the same trees,
Guided by some nucleotide whispers or
A familiar smell in the wind.

You must trust the twisted route,
Over mountain tops, through canals
To find your own familiar.

BIRTH STORY I

Before dawn

The ewe scratches the hay
With her front hoof
Making an opening
To lay and push.

Her lambs will be coming soon.
I watch silently through
The slanted, sacred path
Of barn door sunrays.

On Sunday morning

New life, hungry, drenched
In consecrated waters
Rises on unfamiliar terrain,
Trusts the mother's stern
Bleat, waits for the next
One she knows is coming

Before the day even begins.

FEEDING HOUR

The sheep cluster
Signaled by habitual
Gate and bucket clatters.

I am a daybreak messenger
Of provisions
Barley, oats, and hay.

Liminal, ruminant—
What is left of their wild
Survives by each bite.

I am a witness
Of their ravenous hunger
I am the caretaker
Of their tamed want.

St. Brigid's Day

The sun comes to us
between a break of clouds

and I swirl underneath
the glow until I can no longer

pretend that it is warm.
Snowdrops, bluish nettles,

the soft calls from burrows.
These are just slight

signs of hope revealing
how far we have come.

The ewes are swelling
with milk, almost ready

to burst, a spiral fire burns
in their bellies.

For us, for everything.

THE SHEEP CELEBRATE EARTH DAY

The earth laughs in grass.

Spring pastures arise
From slumber. Ewes grind and ferment
Fresh tips of green blades.
There is a whole concerto in their rumen,
      a four-chambered orchestra
That crescendos with a blatant belch.

In this
Sacred transformation,
Billions of bacteria and protozoa and fungi
Live and die and are reborn as mother's milk.

The flock is focused on the open field.
Browsers by design, sheep will eat all day
Reveling in the land's verdant offering.

They return their own abundance to the soil
In a reciprocal exchange that requires, not thought,
      but a routine belief in their own belonging.

Birth Story II

She extends one noble hoof
like a dancer, for leverage.

A black lamb drops.

Your call came and I answer.
It had been awhile.
Instead of canceling the session
we talk over the phone
about parents and parenting
current joys and frustrations.

Meanwhile another lamb drops,
then another. The experienced
ewe tends to them all. I watch
her diligence as we continue
to examine me. Steam rises
from newly emerged bodies.

This ewe does not need my help
but I need her to teach me
all she knows about animal
bodies and miracles, mothering
and being mothered.

It is the perfect setting, in fact,
for therapy. I am more open
than usual, feeling my way through
the obscure canals of postpartum emotion
as these new lives
join the seasoned flock.

On-Farm Research

The entomologist comes to the farm
to capture and record the diversity
of bees in our fields.

He is trying to find out
how many and what kind
of bees are still here.
How bad is this die-off,
the reported wide-spread hive collapse?

We have a lot of bees here, he tells me,
such as the wool carder bee.
They migrated from England
and collect hairs from plants,
to line their egg cells.
Harvesters of "wool" to cushion
and insulate their young.

We will shear our sheep in September.
I hope to knit my baby a blanket
using their carded and spun wool.
I will wrap it around her
luminous, thin skin in winter.

Our flock grazes beyond the herbs
and vegetables and sweeping motion
of his sword-like net. I watch as the bees,
the scientist, the plants and sheep
do their work. Separate
and also glaringly interwoven.

YEAR OF THE SHEEP

I've watched their tender, pink
Udders swell over the past weeks.
Now they are swollen
To the point of pain.

The lamb drops and is nocturnally
Nurtured to stand. Licked clean
Of all slime and blood.

I have never been so proud to be female.
I have never been so aware of time and place.

Ruminants, living side by side
Grazing day after day
They carry on
As if I am not here. Or,
As if I am not trying
To be here.

We started with five
And now have a flock
Hardy enough to stand
The dank, northwest soil.
Smart enough to avoid the
Sharp barb of bramble
Alongside the field.

According to Chinese astrology,
People born in the year of the sheep
Have special sensitivity to art and beauty
And a fondness for quiet living.

I am carrying my child in my arms.
We are both sheep,
Pointing out the berries and
Dandelion fluff.
She sees the flock amble

Single file back to the barn.
"Baaa!" she says.
"Yes, Baaaa!" I say.
We both see together.
We both smile and wave.

I remember when I wanted to be
Anyone but myself.
When I thought that I had
Everything to prove.

Now my routines are like veins
Inside my own white, pulsing body.
Feed, clean, care, observe.

The work is simple: nurture.

Give attention to someone
Or something that is growing.
Something outside of yourself.

Let your little flock teach you
All you need to know about love.

MOMENTS OF PAUSE

Inspired by "Shepherdess with Her Flock" by Jean-Francois Millet

Red-hooded, she stands
Solitary, patient
Aware of her own
Unawareness. The sheep
Graze behind her,
Backs facing back
Accenting time's irrelevance.

I crave moments like these
When peace and harmony
Seem inevitable. Instead,
It is usually rush and stretch,
Go and scatter.

Some days I stop too,
Cloaked in my synthetic fibers.
But instead of calmly peering
At knitting needles, creating,
I am staring at my smart phone
Desperate for answers to questions
About *lamb eye health,*
Droopy ewes, dewormers
Safe for lactation.

I strive for her contentedness
Though I know it is fleeting,
Those moments of pause when all
You need are sun breaks, fresh
Grass and the passive, soothing
Sighs of your own breath.

BIRTH STORY III

She distanced herself from the herd
by noon. Breathing rapidly, scratching
the hay away to bare sand.
A few hours later, she has leaned
on her full side, lips pursed upwards.
A sure sign of imminent pushing.

The poetry reading started at five
but I was coming early
with all the chairs, refreshments.
Do I leave her?
I hoped for the best, gambled
witlessly on her practiced motherhood.

I read my poems, halfway through
the next reader the picture arrives.
Triplets, healthy, standing,
all attempting to suckle,
safe and healthy for now
as I listen and diligently clap.

The Story of Ruth

I drove this bottle baby
      home in my hatchback,
bleating the whole way.
Her speckled face
      stood out in the sea
      of only white and only brown.

Every morning in the barn
      while the others
      were frantic for food,
she'd curl around my side.
Bottom of the barn hierarchy,
I'd sneak her hay squares
behind the gate,
      to make sure
         she was getting enough.

When I noticed the pox on her
      teats I knew she couldn't
      stay here for much longer—
for fear of infecting them all.

On this cold winter night
      I pray over my kale, bean
      and sausage soup, remembering
that life spawns more life
and what we care for comes
      back to us in hard
      and mysterious ways.

RUTTING RITUAL

Classic head butting   between our rams
Left one with   a bloody skull.
    The fresh red shocks   against the purity of
wool.
    A test of dominance,   rutting never feels
normal.
Sires honoring   themselves
For the spectating   ewes, soon to be expecting.
    They do their job.   The lambs will arrive
in spring.
Three weeks' work   for a year of food and roof.
    They wait patiently   in their pasture

    And count the unbroken days.

BERTHA

She died in her sleep on Ash Wednesday.
Not alone, but separated from the herd.
As flock boss, she did not show weakness.

Oh the girth of her wasn't more than
The worth of her.

She was our first mother,
The first to lamb on this land.
My teacher bellowing 'baas' like Nina
In her deep, soulful way.

Her hefty old frame finally at ease
As we rolled the all of her into a tractor-sized hole.
Remember that you are dust, and to dust you will return.

Sacred, like a white elephant, she will
Stay with us through the soil.

Each root, each new blade.

DREAM OF THE WEST

Last night I dreamt I was grazing on sage brush
And phlox east of the mountains. Then I stammered
Over miles to find
Canyon shelter, river drink.

I wasn't alone, surrounded
By wind and expanse—
Basalt columns that wept at dusk.

My hooves ached in the dry light.
My body sweat under the weight of wool.
Who brought me here to feast and fatten?
Who turned the feral motherland to field?

BIRTH STORY IV

She has put on weight
and regained her glow.
She stands with the rest
of the flock, grazing
on new, lush pasture.
Yet, I am still waiting
for her lambs.
Past due, they are either
alive, dead, or in-utero
mummies, leather shells
of life. All I can do
is watch and wait
a few more days
before we resort
to the thrust
of modern medicine
to force them out.

II. digging

DIGGING UP IRISES

My bearded irises bloomed
in early May. I dug them
up and separated
the corms under
a sweaty sun.

While I worked
I could hear the thumping
of the neighbor son's music.
Then the roar of five teenage
boys in a small aboveground pool.

Irises represent awareness.

I could not see them
but the sounds were as jolting
as when the father lectures his son
about basketball moves or
when the mother frantically mows
at 11 pm with headlights
because God forbid a lawn
covering farmland should
not be longer than a putting green.

I made new spaces
for these tired roots.
I did not complain about the noise.
I kept digging and planting
remembering that the veil
of separation is thin
and life like a rhizome
is resilient and always connected.

The flower speaks: let go.

Eventually the sounds fade
to only whispers buried in my chest;

the conversation that begins
when we turn the world out
and point the spade in.

TWO MOTHERS WALKING

for Anna

We thought they were swans.
Far off shore in a huddle,
lazy swans that chose
to stay.

But the long arc of orange
gave them away. Stragglers,
climate-change refugees
that in a normal year
would never reach
our northern cove
of coastline.

But what is normal anymore?

We were talking
about life and babies. My
daughter, about to walk.
Your daughter, graduating.

You want to clutch
and hold her close, while
mine refuses to be put down.

They grow up so fast, you say.
I need more time to myself, I say.

Driven to near extinction by pollution
these pelicans are a miracle.
                Or an omen.

We stride slowly, like the unfurling tide
acknowledging these visitors
        and the fierce uncertainty
of what may come next.

FENCES

My neighbor has an impeccable lawn,
fit for golf or polo.
In the evening she traverses

the perimeter, picking up
    any imperfections:
Dried leaves, dandelions or embarrassing chickweed.

Our side of the fence is   pasture
lazy with long grasses, clover
    occasional thistles.

While grazing, the sheep study her.
She works linearly past them
on hands and knees
conquering the last moments of   daylight.

This farmland, once tideland
can support many things,
potatoes, wheat,   migrating waterfowl,
the messiness of new life
                pouring out of a ewe at sunset.

I close the barn door, so as not
                to disturb her with the smell of it all.

DIGGING, STILL

I watch the couple bow
To piles of potatoes—
Millet's remorse for not
Lending a hand.
Like Heaney with a pen
Digging ink with wit,
Sometimes we have to unlearn
All that we have been taught
To find our place and our offering.
These working landscapes are idyllic
To the belly of the brush, but obscene
When sweat seeps out the frame
Or down the bind.

TULIP SEASON

Skagit Valley

April is the time of year
When cars flood the fields.

Lookers, cameras, selfie sticks
Huddle under neon umbrellas.

The buried bulbs have waited
Patiently for their brief moment

Of pomp and blossom.
In a few weeks each petal

Will fall into history
Making no noise of their passing.

The green stems will be slashed
Bulbs eventually dug and sold.

The watchers dissipate
Unaware that in the next field
Their next meal is being born.

Eggs

The neighbor's chicken eggs
are dainty ovals, light and smooth
a rainbow of colors
lined up like wishes
in the carton, that cook
up a vibrant, deep yellow, each bite
a delicate gift of fowl flavor.

Our duck eggs are white and wide
thick-shelled and viscous
containing more protein and fat
they fill the gut fast
leaving a gamy glow
on the tongue.
Fuel for the day's work
backbone for the batter
that rises mightily over
the pan.

PINK MOON

Waiting,

for the pink moon to rise.

Lamentable clouds hang low

on the foothills, where snow

lines still linger.

The call of blushing quince

catches my eye.

It's the egg or sprouting grass moon

yet spring is delayed.

I shiver,

in the evening air and notice

that my buoyant snap pea

leaves have been

stripped to stem.

Discouraged,

I turn homeward

seeing the first spring moon

and summer's harvest

only in my expectant mind.

SURRENDER

Sun brings shadows.
Rain brings hope.
The arching cotyledons
Curve towards the light.

Emergence is not earned.

Air cradles in pore space.
Moisture follows gravity.
Light will allow, little seed,
If you let it.

TUSK

Poaching has bred
The tusks out of elephants.

These modified incisors,
Convenient digging sticks,
Might soon be extinct
Followed closely by the species.

Without our tools what are we?

We've left our fellow creatures
Tool-less, toothless
Unable to defend or debark
While our disposable utensils
Form an island in the ocean
Straws, forks, cups, baby everything.

Before kids, I declared
NO PLASTIC!
But, now the house is strewn
With tools that are killing us—

      Though we can't live without.

PLANTING THE HAWTHORN TREE

I brought home the bare root bundle,
From the nursery.

With an almost-ripened baby in my belly
I cannot bend and dig.

I ask my husband to dig a hole,
Hold it straight.

I cannot watch because I am chasing
Our toddler into the barn.

He covers the roots and tamps
Down the tender, spring clods solo.

Later, I confess my disappointment.
I missed the planting.

In truth, I wanted to do it myself.
My hands sanctifying the tree

That will be twenty feet tall
When our girls fledge our nest.

In the reserved dusk light
He unearths the tree and shovels

A new hole. We fill this one together
With hearts and soil on our sleeves.

THE WEASEL AND THE CARPENTER

She carried her babies
One by one, in her mouth
Boldly in broad daylight.

He saw her slip
Through a crack
In the barn wall.

This intrepid mother found
A new home in his wood
Storage racks. Now she flows
Like a ribbon between shelves
Carrying a dead mouse
Back to her clandestine nest.

He hesitates to make eye
Contact, but in his head
He plots a trap packed
With bloody bait.

She is not even trying to hide.

He knows that these
Unpredictable carnivores
Could go after something
Bigger: a duck or a cat.

Despite their small slenderness
They will ferociously clamp
On the spine until their prey
Is left limp and lifeless.

He puts down his hand sander
To rub his own neck
Powdered in dust.

This unapologetic mother
Might just do anything
To protect this year's sneak of kits
Stowed away in the depths
Of his precious bone pile.

FARMERS AT THE MUSEUM

Inspired by William Cumming, Mural of Skagit County Agriculture, 1941

The mural was found in a barn
Now it hangs in a museum
Painted on commission in 1941
By a soon-to-be famous 24-year-old.
The mural depicts the trades of the time:
Logging, Dairy farming
Berry picking, Railroad building.
The slate sky is a thin
Margin over male bodies
Bending, reaching, crouching.
They work in silence,
Facing away from each other
Slender, tan cow hips
Take center, patiently being
Milked. I think about how
These jobs have changed
And how they have not. Just
This morning I was bending
Over to weed a row of parsley,
But new railroads are being stopped.
Berry pickers vote to unionize.
At least one dairy farm has gone robotic.
Still the simplicity of this scene
Settles something in me. The cool,
Natural tones feel like home.
As I leave the museum I run into
A farmer friend who has been
Farming a lot longer than me.
We smile and realize that we are
Both here for the same reason.
I don't recognize him at first.
We are out of the field, out of context.
He just finished delivering
Vegetables to a nearby restaurant.
His hands are coarse.
He smiles honestly.

I could see him hunched
In this mural. Instead he is outside
The painting, in real life, looking
Back in time.

III. familial truths

FIELD GUIDE TO THE BIRDS

A gift from your eldest daughter,
you recorded bird sightings,
your precious feeders
a salvation to the hungry beak.

       I remember the fervid red of cardinals
       against the sleet-gray winter.

Your lead etchings on the margins
are teachings on how to be home
and never too busy to take notes.

Indigo Bunting 7/8/81
Purple Finch 4/19/90
White Crown Sparrow 4/13/2010

A list as long as my life
       of your watchings.
A patience born
       out of circumstance

       and curiosity
for the companionship that arrives
       at the hallowed
           window and perch.

PARIS, FOUR DAYS

Sisters, one in sneakers,
One in heels, navigating
October over stone.
                  Roses and stained glass.
The jabber of years past,
A taste of rabbit and *éclair*.

We had grown apart,
After they fell apart,
In different
                  lives and cities.

The lit and looming beacon
Led us through *arrondissements*
To familial truths
              buried
Under bar smoke and perfume.

The gentle pulse of Metro,

A lullaby.

These golden streets,
A path home to each other.

Visiting Denmark, WI

We searched the cemetery. It was small, half the size of a football field, nestled behind the yellow-stoned Catholic Church and schoolyard. Great-grandfather alongside great-grandmother, well settled. What were their names? A stick marked empty spaces, waiting for matching headstones for son and daughter-in-law. Soulmates that passed within months of each other. We lived too far away to make the back-to-back funerals. Now the ground is frozen solid, hands clenched in the cold. The new marble will arrive when it thaws. Only bones were buried those months before. Their faces are still alive, vivid in my mind. We scour his little hometown for clues: the hardware store, cheese curd factory, antique mall. Finally, we find him, printed in yearbook cartoons and photographs, bound by town records and newspaper clippings in the historical museum's bank basement display. Sometimes you start to know someone better when they are gone, when all that is left are the stories they couldn't tell themselves.

AN APPLETON GIRL RIDES ELEPHANT IN THE CIRCUS PARADE

The clipping says she represented the Red Cross
in the Barnum & Bailey Parade.
I hold the faded image in my hand:

smile, wave, smile, pressed white uniform
atop grey, wrinkled hide.

Her one-story home
on the bank of a creek
was decorated with retired looms,
and stringless violins, a museum
of all her makings. I remember
playing Hi-Ho Cherry-O
before Grandma wheeled
her down the narrow hall
to bathe her, feed her.
The faint smell of cedar
and mint, dust and tired books.

They forgot to mention
she was the first woman
to attend college in her family.
If she had all the opportunities I had,
would she have traded her craft,
the sanctity of her home life,
for a workplace?

Provider or nurturer
mother or maven
or maybe—
we can finally have everything,

Ourselves, in our own parade.
Riding the elephant in the room,
back and forth
        between home and away.

An Elephant With a Mind of Its Own

I still forget things easily these days.
Names, meetings, messages.
Maybe it's baby brain,
Maybe it's not?

*

Nine months--
Plath's ponderous house
Pales against the elephant's
Twenty-two-month gestation.

*

A matriarchy, male elephants live in isolation
From the collective Her. I've tied my trunk to the tail
Of my mother, grandmother, great grandmother
And mother Earth.

*

Elephants are now an endangered species.

*

Back at work
After eight weeks. Pumping,
Packing away the evidence
Of delivery wounds and swell.
Tightening in the sag
Before anyone sees any evidence
Of receptivity.

*

No wonder I can't remember a damn thing.
No wonder mothers, like elephants, sometimes just fade out of
sight.

THE WOOL HOARDER ON CHARITY LANE

Piles of new roving
  bins of untouched yarn.
        All colors and blends:
mohair, cotton, silk,
        A knitting machine
wool picker
carding brushes
skein holder
        and ball winder.
Two spinning wheels,
        a floor loom and middens
of books and patterns.

The women running the sale
were just friends and neighbors.
They didn't knit. She must have been
an artist or about
to open a shop.

I wanted to ask how she died.

Today a young man almost jumped off
the I-5 overpass. He was, thankfully,
talked down by strangers.

After sorting through yarns and patterns
I made myself a small pile.
Overwhelmed by all the color and textures.
Guilty for annexing her unfinished projects.
I am not sure what I will make—
        the yarn was dirt-cheap and soft.

Knitting soothes me,
brings joy and distraction during winter nights.
Mostly, I like the body of wool. The comforting feel
on my hands, its earthy smell.

At home I sort new skeins
with the remains of past projects.
My own yarn stash is growing larger
    each year.
      Larger than I want to admit to anyone.

RECIPE BOX

'It's De-lovely'
Floats from your kitchen
As you turn fat and grain and leaf
Into dinner. I sit in the next
Room and flip through
Index cards in the long tin box.
A life story told by ingredients,
Sauce stains and tattered edges.

The box came back to me
Six years later.

Sage Meatloaf
Tangy Cheese Spread
Good Rhubarb Crumble
Green Bean and Turkey Casserole
Summer Squash Slaw
Strawberry Pie
California Pot Roast

You always served more than enough,
Applauded the empty plate.
Here in the shallow
Light of my kitchen I flip
The cards again
Like they are Tarot,
Predicting my future.

How does this Mother find the time?

Your voice says frankly:
Never skip a step or an ingredient
        And clean, dear one, as you go.

FLECKS OF GRAY

Small wisps
frame my face
dark brown strands
fading translucent
each day
ashen spring clouds
dashed in white
and yellow
swell
with sunlight
and tears
I clench my breath
remembering
how many
fragile days
have passed

Rag Rug

I sort through scraps of fabric
Looking for complimentary colors.
The loom holds warp strands
Under tension to allow interweaving
Of the weft.

The teacher pauses before her demonstration,
Holds a piece of fabric in the air,
Says she believes the first
Piece of any weaving is always
Tethered to an ancestor.

You wove fabric so tight and even,
Fit for table runners or tailored suits.
My rag rug is a beautiful mess
Chunky and thick and uneven.
"Good job for a beginner," she says.

At home, I run my hand over your handiwork.
The red shawl, the yellow napkins
We use at Easter to wipe lamb juice
Off our lips. I rub the texture of it all
Between my fingers, your hours
Of making, the baton of knowledge
That skipped two generations.

Somewhere,
        in my ligaments,
I feel a gentle nod, a pair
Of hands nudging me to try again.
Slow down, collect more scraps—
Lead the line more skillfully
Through the eye.

Night Fire

Boxes of old reports, notes,
Envelopes and wedding rsvp cards
With their blush envelopes burned to ash,
Smoldering alongside severed apple tree
Limbs and unearthed stumps, scrap wood,
Cleared elderberry understory. Inside and outside
We usher change by making space for
New plans and new selves. Under a dark moon,
The fire blazes with loss and relief.
The old shape shifted to smoke and air. The past
Offering warmth over the present chill.

IV. mothering

EPITAPH FOR AN OCTOPUS

When Paul, the prophetic
cephalopod died, I cried.

Beauty is born from a balance
between expansive freedom
and a clear boundary.

Before each game
the Germans hung flags
on each end of his tank.
He would prophesy the winning team
by placing his long, tentacled
arm on the glass.

I forget the spaciousness of living in water,
adhesion always against the skin.
The buoyancy of constant belonging.

I still believe in him, bottom dweller,
even though he is gone.
I covet his three harmonized hearts, titan brain
and easy grace.

My body juts through air
with just these two awkward limbs.
Space along my side for more touch
room left in my chest for more heart.

HER

The spider on the blue drapes
Hangs elusively, unwilling to flinch.

I could kill her or set her free.

She could creep up the curve of my
Neck in the middle of the night
And inject torturous venom. Or,
She could hunt and capture
Our pestering houseflies.

Friend or foe, plain arachnid or grandmother protector?

She continues to hang in perfect
Stillness as I skulk
Behind her in wonder and fear.

ECLIPSED

     Out of the ocean.
Mother lifts limp half-moon
    young.
The grief goes on
    for days.

How we celebrated the passing shadow
    across the sun, yet we neglect

generations of
yin-yang bodies that
arc and sing.

Mysterious tides reflecting sky.

Our sea, now a cauldron of loss
    and plastic.
Our collective future,
    a hazy regret.

FALL SALMON RUN

Samish River, Skagit County

Past the wheat stubble
And spent spinach seed crop
The bridge is littered
With trucks, men and tackle
Boxes awaiting the big Kings
Or maybe the fall Chum-Coho.
Salmon carcasses loll like stones
Along the river floor.
The fall, a last hope
For home.

Farmers and bankers stand shoulder
To tartan shoulder to snag
A wearied one. In water this low,
You could almost yank
A tail by the hand.

I hear a cough and then a
"Fuck!" Two teenage boys
Scramble up from under the
Bridge, coughing, with their trick
Bikes, backpacks, baseball hats
Backwards. They are not in school,
Nor do they see below the water.

To them the salmon is sport.
To the families that paddled
This river first it was spirit food.

When the season was closed,
There was blame on both sides
For the dwindling harvest.
How quickly hate is abandoned
Now that permits are open again.

We are all irreverent teenagers, loitering along the bank,
Watching nameless eddies circle and pass.
Conservation shouldn't cost more than consumption,
But it always does.

PREGNANT EX-PAT IN AN EVERYDAY LANDSCAPE

My world, up close,
Looks strangely familiar.
Apple and pear blossoms
Burst from silent limbs.

> I have the Senator's number
> Memorized: (202) 224-2621.
> I call regularly to voice concern.
> The young, subdued staffer
> Recognizes my voice, listens
> And says, "I'll pass that on."

A robin is bouncing around
Newly planted pea seeds.
Just looking, not taking, I pray.
The rhubarb plant's green mitt
Widens up as if to catch
The sun's original orb.

> Inquiries to the Office of Government Ethics
> From concerned citizens
> Has increased 5200% this year.
> I know I am not alone.

The heart of spring
Holds many contradictions.
Snow still coats the foothills
While tulips and salmonberry blossoms
Expose their frailties to warmer mornings.

> This denial and bullying is not us.
> We've degenerated to
> The shadowy backside of freedom.

I walk barefoot in the cool grass
Embrace my expanded belly,
My own personal march for science

And life and beauty. I sing to
The one I am welcoming to this strange world.

How do I dodge despondency?
Where does my small voice find thunder?

ADAPTATION

Water churns
Around us, a fluid finger
Of the Salish Sea,
Oscillator,
Orchestrator,
Of all near-shore ecologies—
Eel grass, clams, intertidal algae.

Someday,
These waters will rise
Above familiar fence lines,
Into backyard gardens,
Underneath farm fields,
And other unprepared places.

I wonder if I will still be here then.

Perhaps I'll have retreated
Inland to the safety of basalt
And sagebrush—
Safely away from salt
And the buoyancy
Of calling this fragile delta a home.

SWAN

I.

It's makeshift,
an embellished puddle
claiming to be habitat
on dormant farmland.
A wedge of trumpeter swans

migrating

saw it under flight
        and decided to stop.

II.

I called for her at 4 am. I think
it's time. My body is sticky
from the heat, my stretched belly
itches and burns.

Her spirited white Mini Cooper
darts down the driveway.

One centimeter dilated.

Only one.

I sheepishly smile as she holds me
under her graceful wings.

III.

The snow level
dropped last night.
Mount Baker is cloaked
in fresh powder. The foothills, too,
sparkle against waning daylight.
I must stop. I must reach
out from my roadside
roost and take a picture
of this transient flush
of waterfowl.

Mothers and fathers

      and children

anointed by purple sky.

IV.

All day she floated ungrudgingly
between me and the other mother.

Contracting and pushing
screaming and sweating

My hair stuck to my face
sundress soaked,
I soar and breathe
through the pain

while
      she
           welcomes

two journeying souls.

V.

In Houston, after the floods,
a midwife rides an inflatable swan
to reach a laboring client.

Babies don't wait

     for good weather.

Water streamed down her streets, left
her stranded until a neighbor said,

"Try this!"

VI.

I snuggle a giggling girl
in my sweater and sense
the return of the trumpeters.

Soon I will see them
wandering the fields
with their new young.

Sacred

     white

        curves

feasting gratefully
on barley and tuber remains.

VII.

Kindness and fierce flight
guide the wingspan of new life
back to familiar grounds.

It is a calling to birth babies.

Like migration, you must
be ready to answer to
seasons and cycles

and, always,
        always,
            stay the course.

DOG SONG

Last night I heard a banjo tune
that plucked on my own heartstrings.
When I realized it was written
for a lost dog, I cried. Not tears
of joy or sorrow, just damp acceptance
that even the most innocent
of souls can stray.

I think of my own
yellow and golden mix
always loyal and adoring.
The tumor in her liver expands
each month like my belly as her once-portly
build deflates like a birthday balloon.
Her eyes haven't changed, though--
       their glint, a reluctance to leave.

Dog as my teacher
about love and how to nurture.
The new baby arrived
a year ago. Now these
tiny sprite hands
toy with frail paws
tug at smooth ears
tap at her dangling tags.
The soothing chimes echo across
the kitchen. A melody, that reminds me
       I will never be the same.

GHOST BELLY

Baby is unlatching the antique
icebox handle. Unpacking
a week's worth of recycling
from the bin. She moves
freely through the room
on knees and hands
and sometimes feet.

As I bend over to pick
up the shreds of newspaper
and cardboard, I feel
the push of my stomach
against my thigh. Skin
still stretched out
and streaked by her
becoming. Her body once
tethered internally to mine
for all sustenance and spirit.

I cradle this space
where she slept so quietly
for so many years
even when she was only
a hopeful notion.

I probe this empty space
grateful she arrived
not too early or not at all.

I imagine the all-encompassing pain
of disenfranchised grief
that can turn women
into phantom friends,
coveting the other's
expansive growth
before there is enough
time to heal and try again.

TALKING WITH BABIES

"Say Mama."
Silence
"Say Dada."
Finger in mouth.
I know you can do it.
You have done it before.

Today I tried to take her picture
In the garden. Plopped her next
To the thriving chard and kale, for scale.
Tears.
"Just smile," I say.
More tears.
"One quick smile for Mommy."
Wails and sobs.

Her future teenage self whispers in my ear.
"Don't make me do it."
Meanwhile she is putting dirt
Clods in her mouth.

I give up. Inside, I make lunch.
She scarfs it up. As I get up to bring the tiny
Dishes to the sink I hear a "Mama."

I turn and she grins.

WEAN

The day the flow
dwindled
when she promptly
pressed
her supple fingertips
on my nipple
and smiled
I knew she was ready
to be done.
Full of my nectar
a new gossamer
threshold
appeared to both of us.
Before
it was her ululations
that triggered
substantive stream.
Now her winged
giggle makes
us both take ease—
We are side by side
on the couch
under a constellation
of moon, cycle
and sated change.

TREACHEROUS WIND

My daughter coughs in the night.
I am startled, made restless,
by her discomfort.

It's 3 am and I am bottle
feeding an orphaned lamb.
The sides of the barn
crank and moan with each gust,
his little body suckles furiously
for this chance at real life.

Falling back into my safe
and protected bed, I am
haunted by the news of the day;
children, victims in their own
streets, of an unfamiliar,
treacherous wind rendering
bodies limp, mouths
foaming, an unfathomable
atrocity. I feel both guilty
and helpless.

The chimes on the porch score
my grief as the night – winds and all,
passes on to another day.

THE OBJECT

of Impressionism is an accurate
depiction of light and color.

The tea rose hue of Cassatt's *Materinité*,
mother and suckling babe.
A sea of pink and gentle brown sets
my heart pulsing. Makes me believe

that as she learns to swim, fall, run,
she will remember my first invitation
to life, my first real gift that
infused her blood and bones, echoes
bowls full of hope.

Carry-On

I checked my suitcase.
I have one personal item to carry
through the terminal, on the plane.
It's light, almost too light.

I pat the pockets
looking for what's missing.
Ticket, yes. Wallet, yes.
Book that I have been meaning to read, yes.

My hand runs over my stomach,
I feel a fading ache in my breasts.
I never imagined what leaving her
for the first time would feel like.

Rains plasters the tarmac.
I must go, I must never leave you.

EXPECTANT

Lilacs are poised to open
while my gentle pink
peony buds silently swell.
The harsh torrents
of April have dispersed
into a shower or two,
here or there.

May starts tomorrow
and I am ready to welcome
a larger dram of spring.
The ground still gives beneath
my feet, but I have faith
in my next steps, buried
seeds, corms, tubers.

My belly is stretched, again.
My swollen fingers count the days
until Mother's Day,
my birthday and then
                emergence.
Each swift kick and slick hiccup,
a reminder of her readiness,
my ongoing metamorphosis.

You see, change happens
all the time, yet we never
notice until it passes.

Please bring me
ten more toes, ten fingers
and my own heart
opened and willing
to be the mothering me
I am becoming.

RETURNING TO WATER

She enters the water with
trepidation, but this fluid
space absorbs all
of her fears, maybe even
feels like her first true home.

Tiny feet flap
and kick, not
for motion
but investigation
of liminal movement—
her own growing expanse.

The chaos of splash
brings joy and terror
freedom and buoyancy.

She yells, almost cries,
then settles her heart-
shaped lips to the surface
to transform air and water
into effervescent elation.

PRAYER FOR GOOD MOTHERING

I ask for one full day of presence.
when I can dote on her every word
and plea, follow her whimsy
where it leads. No distractions
like phones or bills or errands or chores.
No drifting thoughts about my next
meeting, deadline or creative impulse.

Give me the confidence and faith
that work, in all its infinite forms,
will get done eventually, and well.
This person that I am
and have known for over
thirty-nine years will not
fizzle into oblivion
if I do, in fact, sit on the worn
woven, multi-colored kitchen rug
for hours to build block
kingdoms, roll cars along floor
lines, delight in hiding and finding
the same small figurines.

She shrieks with joy
as we explore the newly
mowed lawn, investigate
freshly turned beds of soil
in the garden. I, too, smile
as the spring sun strikes
my face and warms me
in a new and profound way.

Gratitude

I am grateful to my 2016 Breadloaf/Orion Environmental Writing Workshop cohort and Aimee Nezhukumatathil for initial feedback on poems from this manuscript. Thank you Anna Ferdinand, Adie Smith Kleckner, Melissa Reeser Poulin, and Jo Vance for your support. I am grateful to Margy Lavelle and the i.e. gallery, for opening your doors to poetry and my work. Thank you Susan Rich for teaching on the farm. And Georgia Johnson, you are my hero!

I appreciate Jill McCabe Johnson's guidance and support, and Tina Schumann's masterful edits. Thank you Kary Wayson for your careful read of the final manuscript. Margaret Davidson, I am so honored to have your work on the cover of this book.

My mother, Mary, and my husband, Dean, have offered endless support. To my daughters, June and Eloise—thank you for the joy and wonder you have brought into my life. I love you all!

And to my ever-growing flock, thank you for all you offer.

Acknowledgments

Poems previously published include:

"Fetal Movement"
>   *All We Can Hold: An Anthology of Poems About Motherhood,* Sage
>   Hill Press
"Dog Song"
>   *Poets on the Coast Anthology*
"Tulip Season"
>   *WA 129+* Digital Chapbook, Sage Hill Press
"Pregnant Ex-Pat in an Everyday Landscape," "Fall Salmon Run"
>   *About Place Journal*
"Moments of Pause"
>   *Ekphrastic Review*
"Year of the Sheep"
>   *Pilgrimage*
"Night Fire"
>   *Magnolia Review*
"Ghost Belly"
>   *Snapdragon*
"On-Farm Research"
>   *The Hopper*
"Fleece"
>   *Orion Magazine*
"Prayer for Good Mothering"
>   *Mothers Always Write*
"Eclipsed"
>   *For Love of* Orcas, Wandering Aengus Press
"Latch"
>   *(m)othering* anthology, Inanna Press
"Adaptation" & "Farmers at the Museum"
>   *Cascadia Rising Review*
"Two Mothers Walking" & "Digging Up Irises"
>   *Mycorrhizae*

About the Author

Jessica Gigot is a poet, farmer, teacher, and musician. She operates a small farm in Bow, Washington called Harmony Fields that makes artisan sheep cheese and grows organic herbs. Jessica has lived in the Skagit Valley for more than fifteen years and is deeply connected to the artistic and agricultural communities that coexist in this region. Her first book of poems, *Flood Patterns*, was published by Antrim House Books in 2015. *Feeding Hour* is her second poetry collection. Her writing appears in several publications, including *Orion*, *Taproot*, *Gastronomica*, *The Hopper*, and *Poetry Northwest*.

CPSIA information can be obtained
at www.ICGtesting.com
Printed in the USA
LVHW030750301120
672995LV00006B/416